Consider

THIS NOTEBOOK AS YOUR COMPANION TO EXPLORE THE WONDERS OF NORTHAMPTONSHIRE.

Use it to help guide you through your personal journey of the county. Make notes and doodle your way through the book as you learn all the amazing facts that Northamptonshire has to offer.

NORTHAMPTON MUSEUM has 13,000 pairs of shoes, which is the largest collection of shoes in Europe.

SHOES MADE
IN NORTHAMPTONSHIRE
ARE WORN ALL OVER THE WORLD

NENE VALLEY NATURE BINGO

Covering more than 41,000 hectares, Nene Valley is home to some of the most spectacular views and stunning landscapes that Britain has to offer. An oasis of tranquillity, Nene Valley is the perfect place for adventure, discoveries and becoming one with nature.

Play nature bingo by marking off all the animals and creatures on the page. We have given you a head start with the bumblebee.

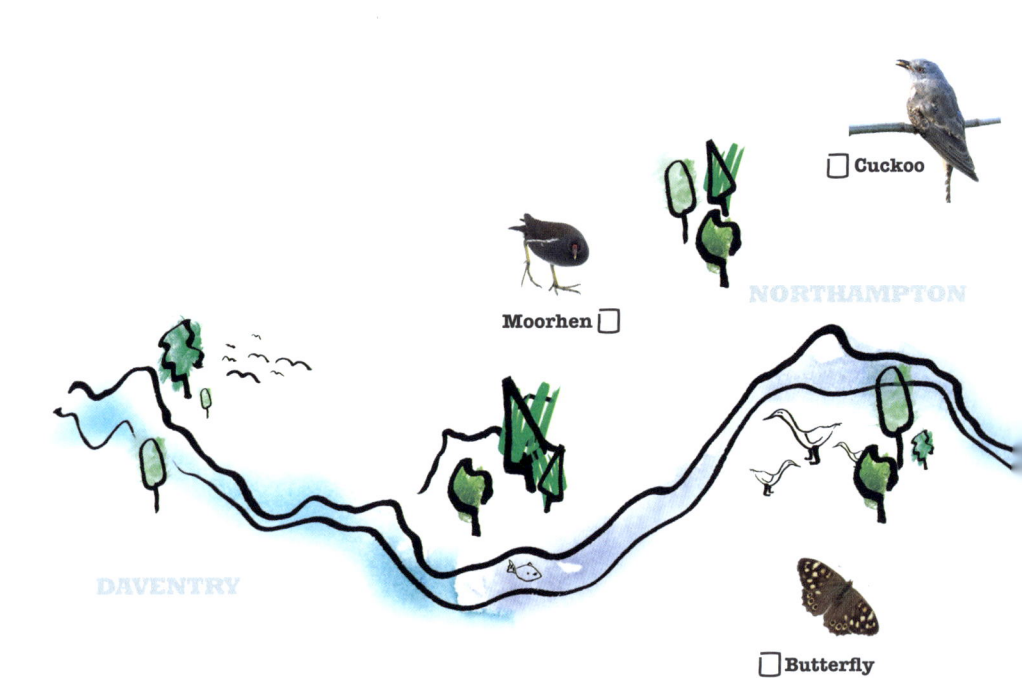

Bumblebee ✓

☐ Cuckoo

Moorhen ☐

NORTHAMPTON

DAVENTRY

☐ Butterfly

☐ Red Kite

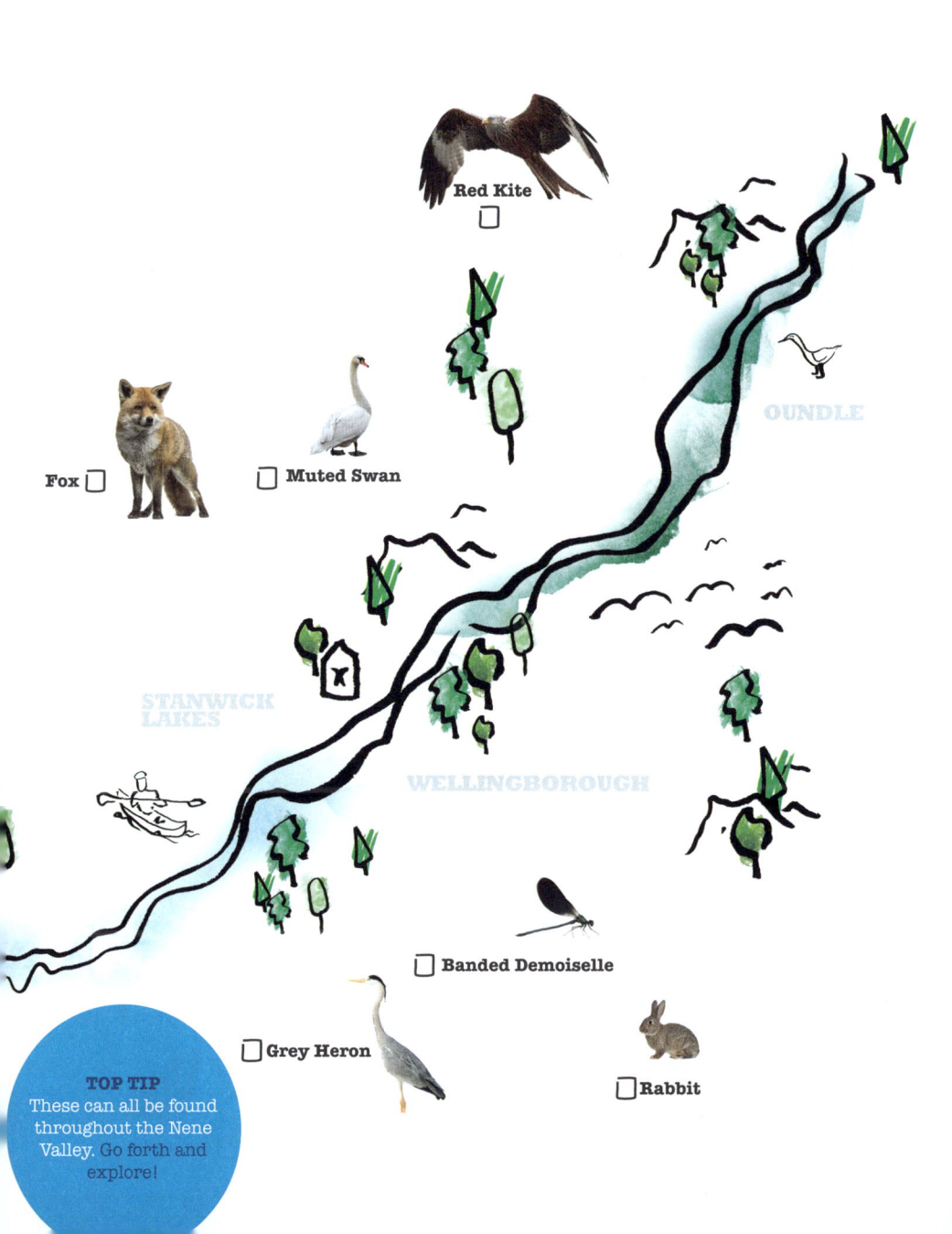

☐ Fox

☐ Muted Swan

OUNDLE

STANWICK LAKES

WELLINGBOROUGH

☐ Banded Demoiselle

☐ Grey Heron

☐ Rabbit

TOP TIP
These can all be found throughout the Nene Valley. Go forth and explore!

ONLY FOR HARD NUTS

— The WORLD CONKER CHAMPIONSHIPS are held in Northamptonshire every year. Only the bravest of souls, and the hardest nuts from around the globe compete for the title of King and Queen Conker.

More information can be found at: www.worldconkerchampionships.com

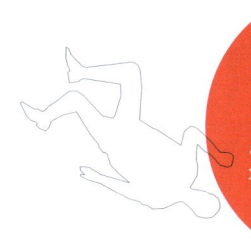

DID YOU KNOW?
The only Prime Minister to be assassinated came from Northampton

— SPENCER PERCEVAL, was shot in the lobby of the House of Commons in 1812 by John Bellingham.

SOLVE THE SECRET OF LIFE

- Scientist Sir Francis Crick was born in Northampton in 1916. With James D Watson he discovered the structure of DNA and was awarded a joint Nobel Prize in 1962.

In 2005 a public sculpture called **Discovery**, which was created by Lucy Glendinning, was erected in Abington Street to commemorate his life.

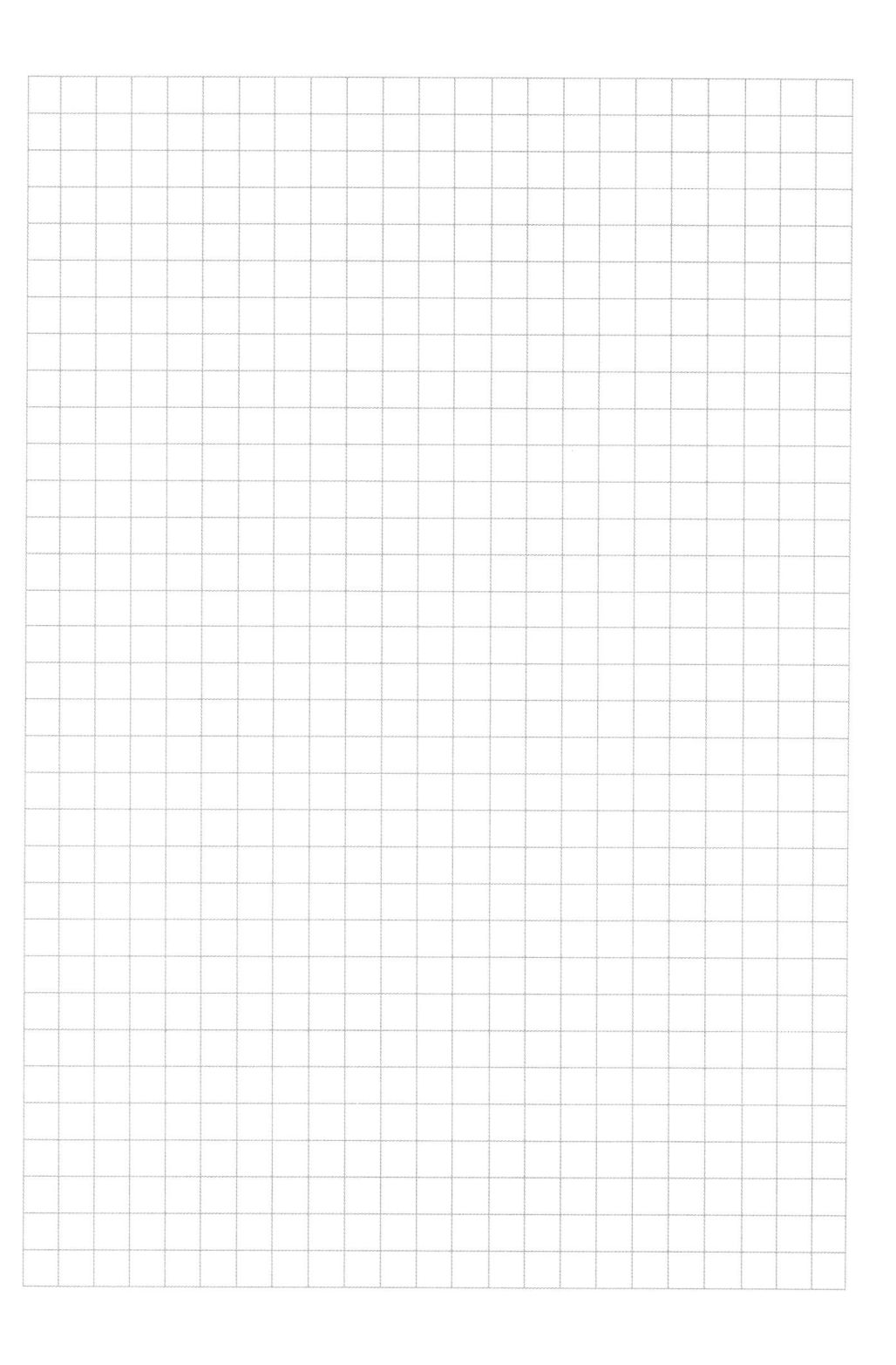

WHAT CAME FIRST? THE CHICKEN OR THE EGG?
- NORTHAMPTONSHIRE'S PRODUCE IN NUMBERS

As a rural county at the heart of the country, Northamptonshire is renowned for its home grown foods from brewing to baking and everything in between.

Northamptonshire also hosts The annual Carlsberg UK Northamptonshire Food and Drink Awards that celebrates the finest producers, chefs, restaurants and pubs in the county.

687 million loaves of bread could be made each year from all the barley that is grown within Northamptonshire

365 million pints of beer could be made from all the barley that is grown in the county

300 million eggs are produced in Northamptonshire's poultry farms every year

65 million litres of milk are produced every year by Northamptonshire cows

4,000+ people are employed by the farming sector in Northamptonshire

77% of the land in Northamptonshire is farmland.

525 MILLION
GREEN BOTTLES SITTING ON THE WALL...

♥ LOVE NORTHAMPTONSHIRE

www.love-northamptonshire.co.uk

CARLSBERG'S NEW BOTTLING FACILITY IN NORTHAMPTON PRODUCES ROUGHLY:

60,000 BOTTLES PER HOUR

10 MILLION BOTTLES PER WEEK

AND A STAGGERING **525 MILLION** BOTTLES PER YEAR

IF YOU PUT THOSE 525 MILLION BOTTLES END TO END, YOU'LL STRETCH AROUND THE EARTH 2.48 TIMES.

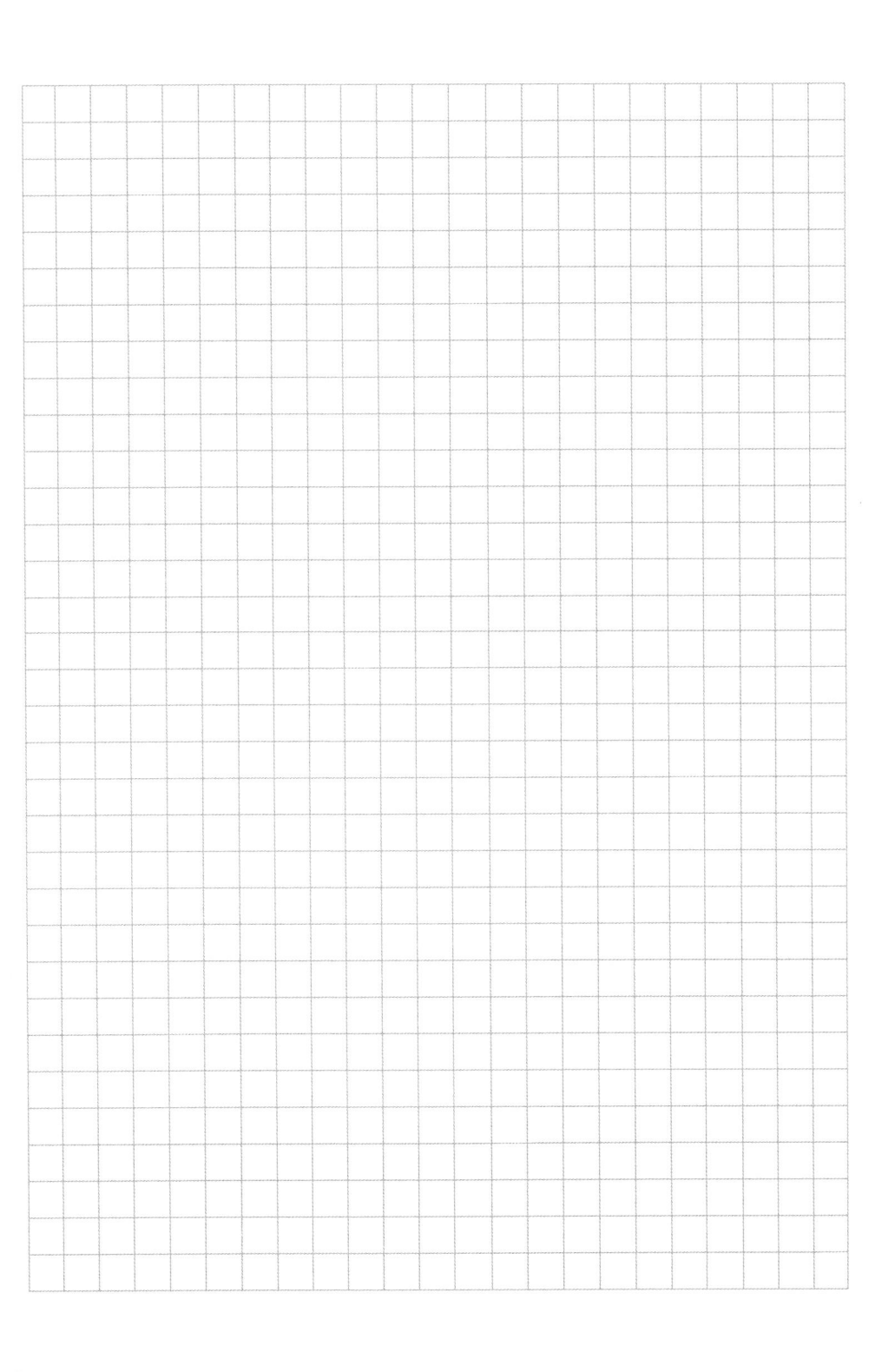

The Gunpowder Plot of 1605, which in earlier centuries was often called the Gunpowder Treason Plot or the Jesuit Treason, was a failed assassination attempt against King James I of England and VI of Scotland by a group of provincial English Catholics, led by Robert Catesby.

GUN POWDER PLOT

PLANNED AT ASHBY ST. LEDGERS MANOR IN NORTHAMPTONSHIRE

Silverstone
in numbers

231 kph
5.891 km
52
1

- Silverstone is one of the longest standing Grand Prix Venues. Here are a couple of things you might not know!

1 priest invaded the track during a race. He was later sentenced to two months in jail

is the circuit length

laps are completed per race

is the average speed F1 cars travel round the Silverstone track

1950 was the year that Silverstone held the first round of the Formula 1 World Championship

1:30.874 is the lap record which was set by Fernando Alonso in 2010

300,000 people attend the three day British Grand Prix

The Hart on the left hand side of the crest represents the royal forests in the county: Rockingham, Salcey and Whittlebury.

The Falcon represents King Edward III's link to the county.

The Bull on the right hand side of the crest represents Northamptonshire's world famous shoe & leather industry,

The chain around the neck of the hart represents the steel industry in Northamptonshire.

ROSA · CONCORDIAE · SIGNUM

'Rosa Concordiae Signum' is the county motto. It translates to 'The Rose: The Emblem of Harmony'

The rose in the centre of the crest represents Northamptonshire's involvement in the war of the roses. The rose has been the emblem of Northamptonshire since 1665.

OUR COUNTY CREST EXPLAINED

Ever wondered the story behind our county's crest? Wonder no more. Everything you need to know is right here.

WHAT WOULD YOUR CREST LOOK LIKE?

If you were to design a crest that represented you, what would it look like? **Design your own crest below and see how it compares to ours.**

DID YOU KNOW?
Princess Diana's final resting place is at her family home, Althorp House, which is located in Northamptonshire.

- The Spencer family have lived at Althorp House for 19 generations. Diana is buried on an island in the middle of the lake.

3500BC
FIRST SETTLEMENTS APPEARED AT BRIAR HILL

400BC
HILLFORT BEGAN AT HUNSBURY HILL

43AD
THE ROMANS ARRIVED IN NORTHAMPTONSHIRE

2000BC
BRONZE AGE ROUND BARROWS (ARCHAEOLOGICAL MONUMENTS) WERE FOUND ACROSS NORTHAMPTONSHIRE

1011AD
NORTHAMPTONSHIRE RECORDED AS COUNTY OF HAM TUNN

878AD
WATLING STREET WAS ESTABLISHED AS THE DANELAW BOUNDARY

1086AD
THE DOMESDAY BOOK WAS THE FIRST COMPREHENSIVE CENSUS OF ENGLAND

1605AD
GUNPOWDER PLOT PLANNED AT ASHBY ST. LEDGERS

1631AD
POET JOHN DRYDEN WAS BORN IN THE VILLAGE OF ALDWINCLE

1607AD
NEWTON REBELLION PROTESTED AGAINST ENCLOSURES

1645AD
BATTLE OF NASEBY

1675AD
GREAT FIRE OF NORTHAMPTON DESTROYED THREE QUARTERS OF THE TOWN

1647AD
CHARLES I, HELD PRISONER AT HOLDENBY HOUSE

1780AD
THE ANTI-SLAVERY CAMPAIGNER, IGNATIUS SANCHO WHO MAY HAVE SPENT TIME AT BOUGHTON HOUSE, DIED

1796AD
THE GRAND JUNCTION CANAL TO BLISWORTH OPENED

NORTHAMPTONSHIRE TIMELINE

FIND OUT MORE: WWW.NORTHAMPTONSHIRETIMELINE.COM

1380AD — THE LAST PARLIAMENT TO ASSEMBLE AT NORTHAMPTON

1290AD — ELEANOR OF CASTILE, THE QUEEN CONSORT OF EDWARD I, DIES

1131AD — HENRY I CALLS PARLIAMENT AT NORTHAMPTON CASTLE

1164AD — TRIAL OF THOMAS A BECKET AT NORTHAMPTON CASTLE

1437AD — ELIZABETH WOODVILLE, WIFE OF EDWARD I, BORN AT GRAFTON REGIS

1587AD — EXECUTION OF MARY QUEEN OF SCOTS AT FOTHERINGHAY CASTLE

1460AD — SECOND BATTLE OF NORTHAMPTON IN THE WARS OF THE ROSES

1540AD — BIRTH OF CHRISTOPHER HATTON, LORD CHANCELLOR UNDER ELIZABETH I

1765AD — NORTHAMPTON MERCURY REPORTS PROTEST AGAINST ENCLOSURES

1678AD — SESSIONS HOUSE AND COUNTY HALL IN GEORGE ROW COMPLETED

OPEN ME FOR THE NORTHAMPTONSHIRE TIMELINE

1808 AD
BIRTH OF CAROLINE CHISHOLM (NEE JONES), HUMANITARIAN

1854 AD
CHARGE OF THE LIGHT BRIGADE LED BY JAMES BRUDENELL

1857 AD
MECHANISATION COMES TO THE BOOT AND SHOE INDUSTRY

1910 AD
WALTER TULL TRANSFERS TO NORTHAMPTON FOOTBALL CLUB

1880 AD
CHARLES BRADLAUGH, POLITICAL ACTIVIST, ELECTED MP FOR NORTHAMPTON

1905 AD
THE RAUNDS MARCH

1943 AD
MAJOR CLARK GABLE FLIES COMBAT MISSIONS FROM POLEBROOK

1948 AD
BRITISH GRAND PRIX FIRST HELD AT SILVERSTONE

1959 AD
OPENING OF THE M1, THE FIRST 'FULL LENGTH' MOTORWAY

2003 AD
FIRST CHIP & PIN TRIALS IN THE UK HELD IN NORTHAMPTON

2014
SILVERSTONE WILL HOLD ITS 50TH F1 GRAND PRIX

2014
WOMEN'S TOUR OF BRITAIN STARTS IN OUNDLE

1793 AD
POET JOHN CLARE WAS BORN IN HELPSTON

1796 AD
SPENCER PERCEVAL, WHO WENT ON TO BECOME PRIME MINISTER IN 1809 ELECTED MP FOR NORTHAMPTON

1803 AD
MISSIONARY AND EMANCIPATOR, WILLIAM KNIBB, BORN IN KETTERING

1916 AD
SCIENTIST FRANCIS CRICK WAS BORN IN NORTHAMPTON

1918 AD
WORLD WAR 1 FLYING ACE MAJOR EDWARD MANNOCK, WHO BECAME SECRETARY OF THE WELLINGBOROUGH INDEPENDENT LABOUR PARTY, DIED

1917 AD
BASSETT LOWKE MOVED INTO 78 DERNGATE WHICH IS NOW KNOWN AS 'THE MACKINTOSH HOUSE'

1934 AD
WORK BEGAN IN CORBY ON THE LARGEST STEELWORKS IN BRITAIN

1923 AD
MARGARET BONDFIELD WAS ELECTED MP FOR NORTHAMPTON

2009 AD
HEAVIEST SNOWFALL IN 20 YEARS

2005 AD
NORTHAMPTONSHIRE FEATURED IN TWO FILMS, KINKY BOOTS AND PRIDE AND PREJUDICE

2013 AD
A ROMAN MOSAIC GOES ON PERMANENT DISPLAY AT STANWICK LAKES, AFTER UNDERGOING £10,000 RESTORATION PROJECT

2012
THE OLYMPIC TORCH RELAY PASSED THROUGH NORTHAMPTONSHIRE

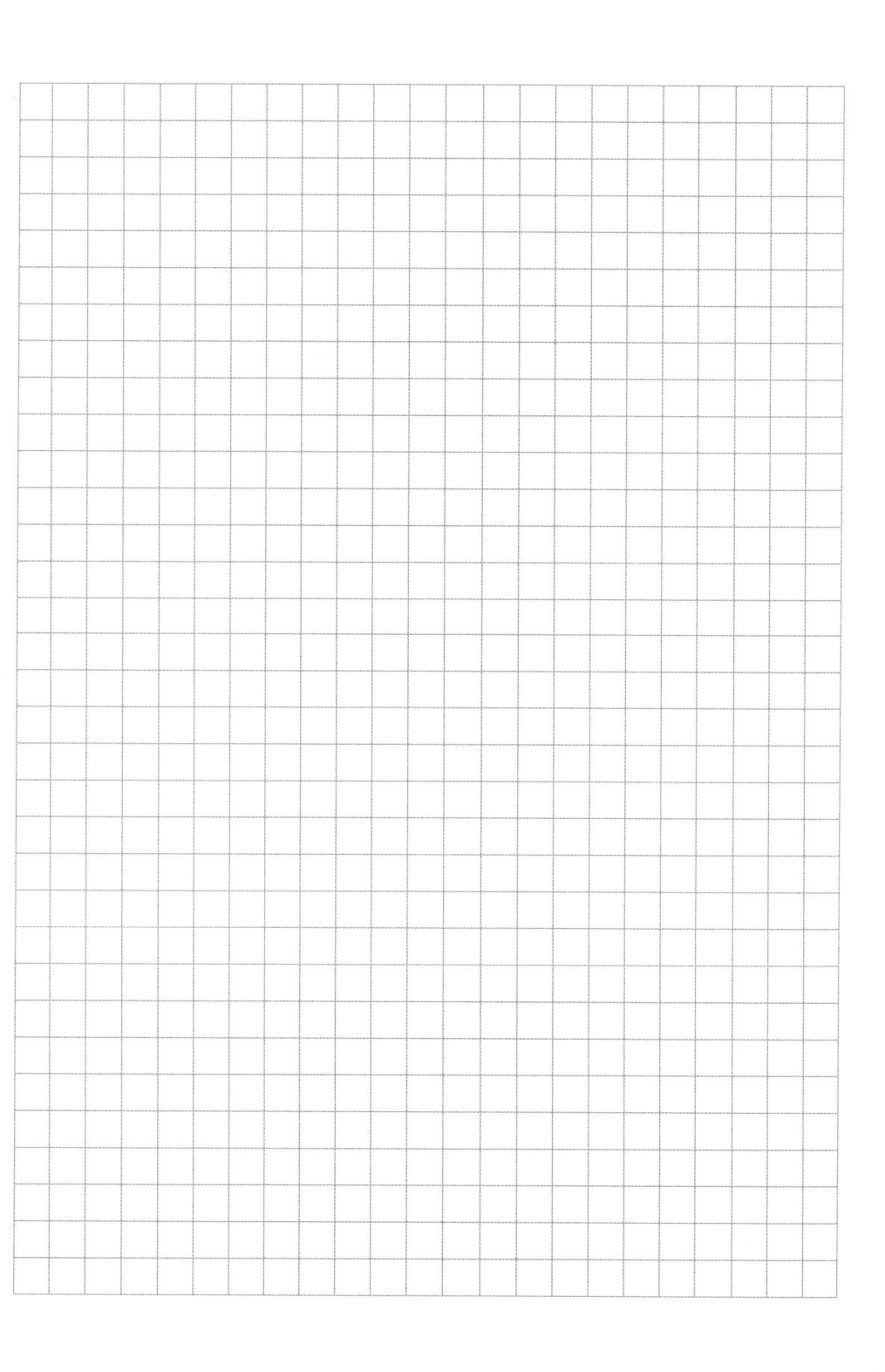

As well as making shoes, Northamptonshire was also the filming location of choice for **KINKY BOOTS!**

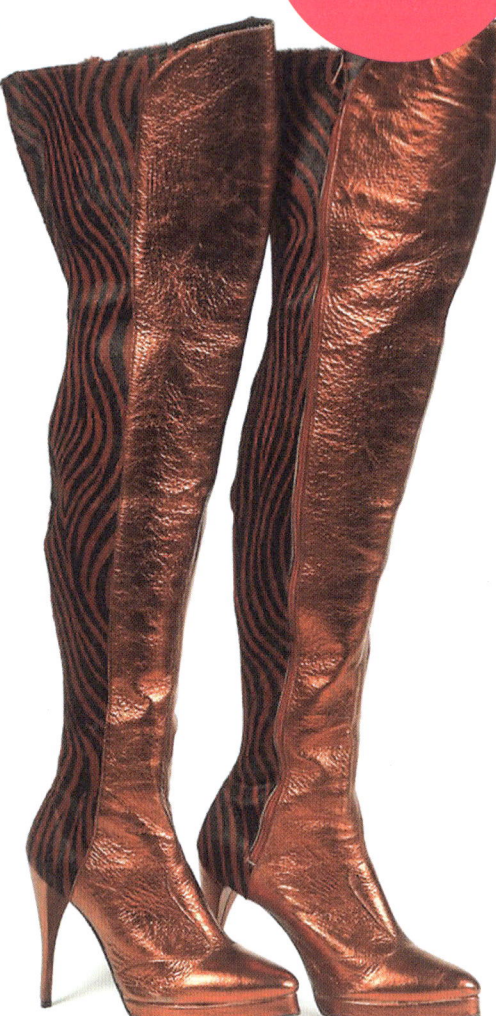

NORTHAMPTONSHIRE has a history of producing some of the most iconic and elaborate shoes in the world.

Northampton first started making shoes in the 15th Century and by 1841 there were 1,821 shoemakers in the town. Northampton Museum and Art Gallery is home to the national collection of shoes, which contains 12,000 shoes dating from 1620.

Highlights of the collection include a pair of white satin shoes which were worn by Queen Victoria on her wedding day in 1840 and a large pair of Dr Marten stilt's which were worn by Sir Elton John as Pinball Wizard in the rock opera film Tommy.

Because of its shoe fame, Northamptonshire was the chosen location for the 2005 movie Kinky Boots, which told the tale of a shoe maker who turned to producing fetish footwear.

DRAW YOUR OWN PAIR OF SHOES

CREATE your own pair of elaborate or crazy shoes!

WHO FROM NORTHAMPTONSHIRE SAVED THE WORLD FROM DALEKS WITH A JAMMY DODGER?

ANSWER: MATT SMITH

MORE DOCTOR WHO FROM NORTHAMPTONSHIRE

1 *Delia Derbyshire,* who helped create the famous Doctor Who theme tune, spent the last 20 years of her life living in Northampton. It was one of the first TV themes to be created entirely electronically.

2 *Tom McRae,* who wrote the two-part story *Rise of the Cyberman* and *Age of Steel* for the 2006 series, grew up in Weedon Bec.

3 The 1977 Doctor Who episode 'The Talons of Weng Chan' starring Tom Baker as the Time Lord was filmed at the *Royal Theatre* in Northampton.

4 Best known for their tweed jackets, Montague Jeffery — a Northamptonshire company that has been in operation for 112 years - *has designed some of the clothes worn by the Time Lord himself.*

5 Barry Nobel, who played one of the original *Cybermen* during the fourth series in 1963, now lives in Kettering.

Chester Farm in Wellingborough is an archaeological and historically important site which stretches over 34 hectares. It has been given scheduled monument status, which means it is protected against unauthorised change. Several Grade II and Grade II* listed buildings can also be found there too.

Evidence suggests that there was human activity on site 10,000 years ago and it is believed to have been home to many different communities over the years.

KEY

Enclosure **E**
Ditch **D**
Building **B**
Temple **T**
Gateway **G**
Public Open Space **O**

Evidence of occupation and activity on site include:

- Mesolithic flint found supports evidence of activities carried out by hunter gatherers.

- Iron age farm.

- Roman walled town, roads, temples and domestic buildings.

- A deserted medieval village which is known as Chester-by-the-Water, including the open field system.

- Post medieval farm complex with a range of buildings dating from the 16th/17th century through to the 20th century.

- Tramway used for ironstone extraction in the late 19th century and early 20th century.

ROMAN TOWN AT CHESTER FARM

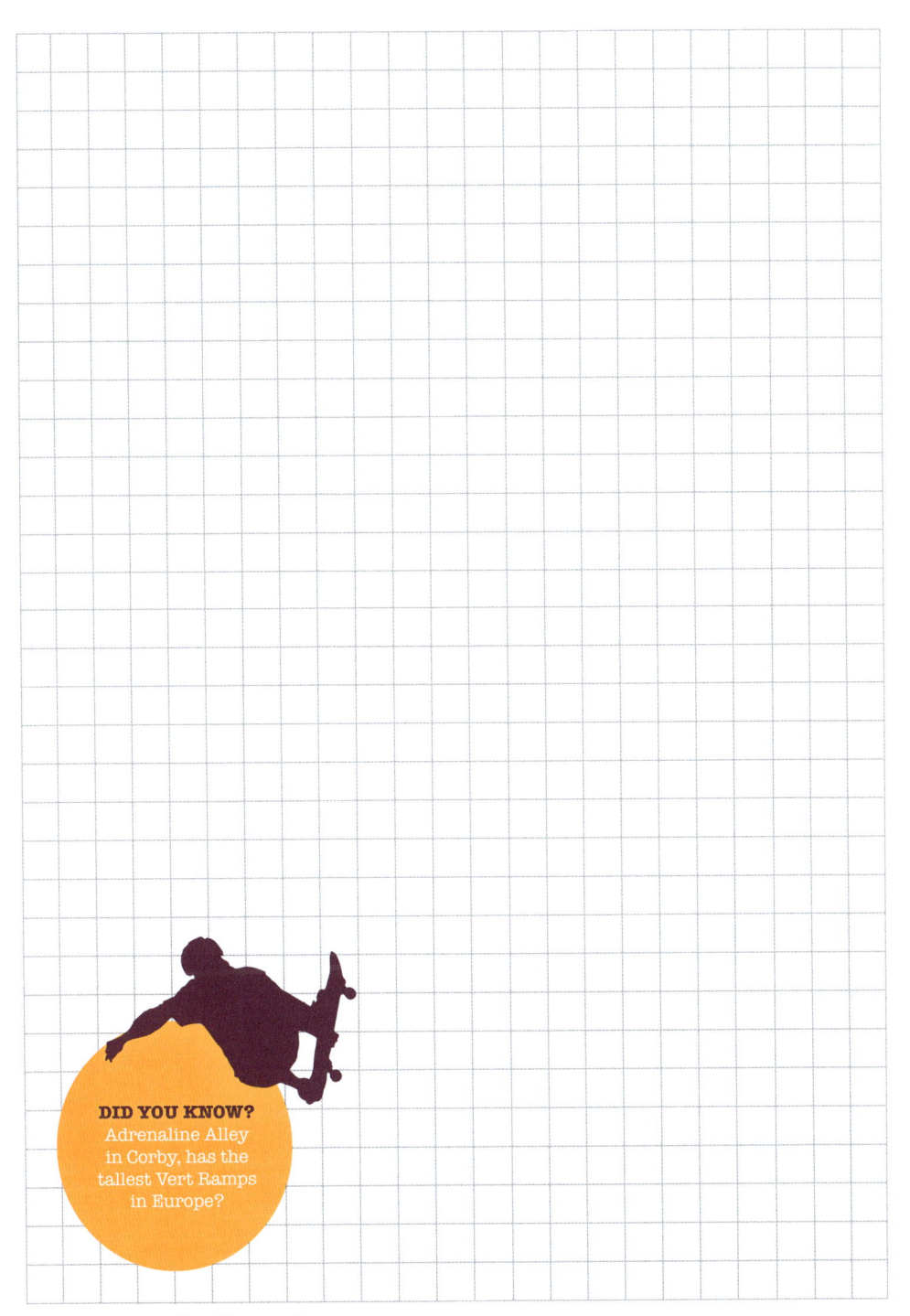

DID YOU KNOW?
Adrenaline Alley in Corby, has the tallest Vert Ramps in Europe?

www.adrenalinealley.co.uk

NORTHAMPTONSHIRE'S 10 POINT PLAN

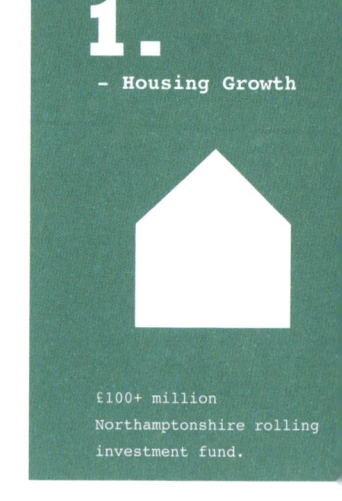

1.
- Housing Growth

£100+ million Northamptonshire rolling investment fund.

In 2012, Northamptonshire was named the most enterprising place in Britain, an accolade we are very proud of. Our work is not done and we have ambition for the future of our county.

The 10 Point Plan is our growth proposition to central government. Our vision is that Northamptonshire will continue to build on the success stories of the past few years and place itself firmly on the national and international business map.

As part of the plan we want to help create **70,000 new jobs** here in Northamptonshire over the next 15 years and provide the infrastructure which could potentially release over **80,000 new homes.**

FIND OUT MORE:
www.northamptonshire.gov.uk

2. - Digital Economy
Superfast broadband for Northamptonshire.

3. - Innovation
Helping innovative local businesses to grow.

4. - High Performance Technologies (HPT)
Stimulating the growth and development of the HPT sector.

5. - Logistics & Distribution
Supporting innovation, reducing congestion and creating new jobs.

6. - Public Sector Land & Buildings
Regeneration and consolidation of assets, new houses and jobs.

7. - International Investment & Trade
Attracting more international trade and investment to Northamptonshire.

8. - Energy Efficiency
Northamptonshire aspiring to become the leading low-carbon location in Britain.

9. - Civic Infrastructure
Delivering world class infrastructure for communities and business.

10. - Skills and Employment
Reducing unemployment and increasing job prospects.

A WORD IN ERNEST IS AS GOOD AS SPEECH

CHARLES DICKENS
BLEAK HOUSE

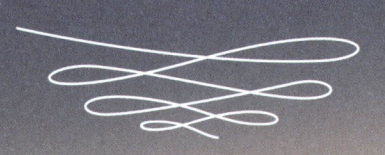

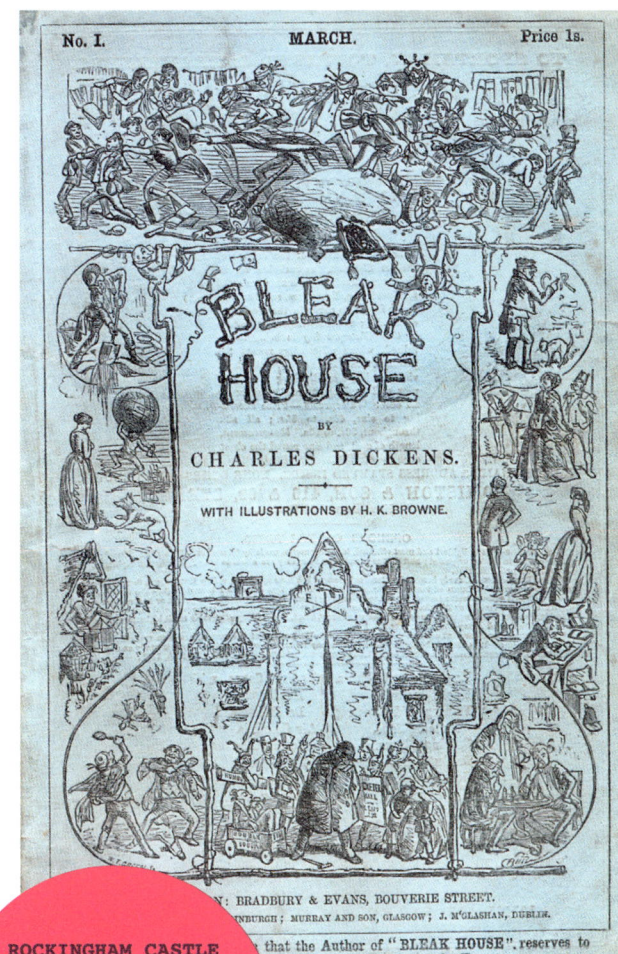

The castle, which dates back to the 11th century, was built on the instruction of William the Conqueror, shortly after the Norman Invasion of Britain. **The original castle was made up of wood and stone, known as a motte and bailey structure, before William II later replaced it completely using just stone.**

WWW.ROCKINGHAMCASTLE.COM

ROCKINGHAM CASTLE was a famous haunt of author Charles Dickens. It was also Chesney Wold's inspiration for his most famous work, Bleak House.

ROCKINGHAM CASTLE HAS ALSO BEEN A FAMILY HOME FOR OVER 450 YEARS

It was during the Tudor period that Henry VIII gave the castle to Edward Watson, who was ancestor to the present owners, the Watson's.

NORTHAMPTON ALIVE

Regenerating Northampton one brick at a time. From creating a new train station and bus interchange to planning a brand new university campus and restoring old breweries into new ones, Northampton is alive with ambition.

Alive Projects. Some of the changes include creating a new art-house cinema and improving the Cultural Quarter, building new offices, student accommodation and a skate park, and rejuvenating the Saints rugby ground making it even better than it already is.

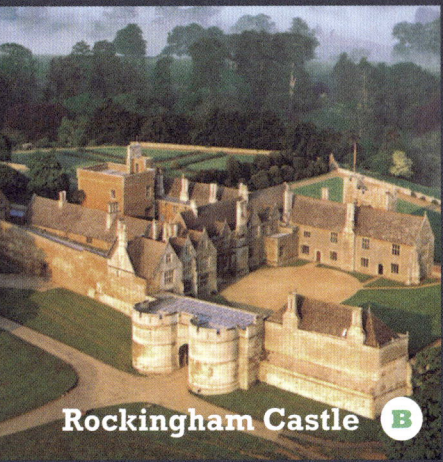

A BRIEF GUIDE TO THE NORTHAMPTONSHIRE COUNTRYSIDE

Why not explore our magnificent countryside. We've even listed a few places for you to start.

A Pitsford Reservoir

B Rockingham Castle

C Lyveden New Bield

D Fotheringhay Church

E Salcey Forest

– THE TOP SECRET, psychedelic, diverse and unique festival Shambala takes place in Northamptonshire every year. It has been voted one of the top three most family friendly festivals in the UK.

Find out more:
www.shambalafestival.org

SHAMBALA

FROM ITALY TO NORTHAMPTONSHIRE AND BACK AGAIN

Olives are one of Italy's most famous exports. Olives are one of the main ingredients of a vodka martini, favoured by James Bond. Pierce Brosnan wore Church's shoes during his adventures as the 007 agent. Church's has been based in Northampton since 1873 and is owned by Prada, the luxury Italian design house.

CHURCH'S MAKE **5000** PAIRS OF SHOES A WEEK

70% OF WHICH ARE EXPORTED AROUND THE WORLD

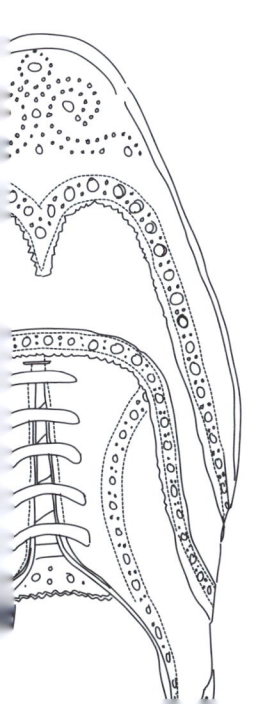

THE FUTURE KING OF ENGLAND PRINCE WILLIAM AND BROTHER PRINCE HARRY **PROUDLY WEAR CHURCH'S SHOES.** AS DO MANY OTHER INTERNATIONAL ROYALS AND NATION LEADERS.

ELIZABETH HALL,
GRANDDAUGHTER OF WILLIAM SHAKESPEARE; THE GREAT BARD, LIVED IN ABINGTON PARK MANOR, NORTHAMPTON FROM 1642.

You can find her grave in the Abington Park Church Cemetery

ABINGTON PARK MANOR
NORTHAMPTON

OUNDLE IN NORTHAMPTONSHIRE WILL
HOST THE START OF THE FIRST WOMEN'S
CYCLE TOUR OF GREAT BRITAIN IN 2014

A RIDE FOR

START
Oundle

Corby

Desborough

Brigstock

Geddington

Kettering

Brixworth

Wellingborough

FINISH
Northampton

THE AGES

– INFLUENTIAL AUTHOR ALAN MOORE, who penned V For Vendetta and Watchmen among others, was born and still lives in Northampton.

FAMILY WEEKENDER

Inspiration for a family weekender in Northamptonshire

SATURDAY

Saturday Morning

Nene White Water Centre
Get your wetsuit on and bounce down the rapids at Northamptonshire's premiere water sport venue.

www.nenewhitewatercentre.co.uk

Saturday Lunch

Nana's Kitchen, Northampton
One of the most popular places to grab a bite to eat in the town.

www.mostmarvellous.co.uk

Saturday Afternoon

Salcey Forest Tree Top Walk
See all the wildlife Northamptonshire has to offer from a new perspective on the Tree Top Walk.

www.forestry.gov.uk/salceyforest

Royal & Derngate Theatre
This multi-purpose venue is best known for holding an eclectic mix of theatre, opera, live music, dance and comedy shows.

Saturday Evening

www.royalandderngate.co.uk

SUNDAY

The Granary Hotel
Visit the idyllic, family friendly hotel for a comfortable night's sleep set within the peaceful countryside.

Saturday Night
www.granary-hotel.com

Sunday Morning
www.llamatrekking.co.uk

Catangaer Llama's
Take a trip to Towcester's llama farm, where the kids can take part in llama treks and learn all about these fascinating creatures.

Sunday Lunch

Courtyard Café, Daventry
A perfect spot for an effortless family lunch.

www.thecourtyardcafe.org.uk

Sunday Afternoon

Cycling, Pitsford Reservoir
Rent a bike at Pitsford so you can cycle round the reservoir, taking in the stunning landscapes the area has to offer.

www.pitsfordcycles.co.uk

FINISH

From a couple of hours to several days and beyond, Northamptonshire has lots to keep you and the family entertained all year round.

PERFECT DAY FOR ART LOVERS

Northampton Museum and Art Gallery
Explore the extensive collection of art and shoes which all have an interesting and unique history behind them.

Morning
www.northampton.gov.uk/museums

Lunchtime

The Dining Room at 78 Derngate
Sample the culinary delights that the only Charles Mackintosh house outside Scotland has to offer.

www.78derngate.org.uk

Afternoon

Fermynwoods Contemporary Art
This independent arts organisation has been commissioning artists and increasing art awareness across Northamptonshire and beyond for 15 years.

www.fermynwoods.co.uk

Errol Flynn Filmhouse
Northampton's unique filmhouse promises the discerning moviegoer an affordable and exciting experience.

Evening
www.errolflynnfilmhouse.com

FINISH

From the world's greatest collection of shoes to the most varied selection of stage entertainment, Northamptonshire has proven it is an inspiring and artistic place to visit.

PERFECT DAY FOR HERITAGE LOVERS
TAKE A STROLL THROUGH TIME

Canal Museum, Stoke Bruerne
A treasure trove of stories, films, working boats, traditional clothing and canal crafts can be found at Stoke Bruerne's museum.

Morning
www.canalrivertrust.org.uk

Morning

Northampton Castle
Explore the history within the walls of one of the most famous Norman castles in England. In 1164, Thomas A Becket was tried at the castle before a great council.

Lunchtime

Church of St Mary and All Saints, Fotheringhay
Completed in 1430, many people visit the church to see the 15th-century painted pulpit which was donated by Edward IV.

Afternoon

Naseby Battlefield
Visit the historic site where the Battle of Naseby took place. Many historians believe that after Hastings and the Battle of Britain, Naseby was the most important and decisive battle ever fought in England.

www.battlefieldstrust.com

FINISH

Rockingham Castle
The castle is steeped with history and visitors will understand why William the Conqueror chose the site for it to be built because of the magnificent views overlooking the Welland Valley.

Evening
www.rockinghamcastle.com

PERFECT DAY FOR ADRENALINE JUNKIES

Northampton Skate Park
Dig out your skateboard for a high energy ride at Northampton's skate park where you are guaranteed to get your heart pumping.

Morning

Lunchtime

Silverstone Circuit
Take to the tarmac on the greatest motorsport circuit in the world as part of the special car experience and track days that are available to participate in.

www.silverstone.co.uk

Afternoon

Grendon Lakes
If wakeboarding and paintballing are your thing, then get yourself down to Grendon for a session on the lake and some adrenaline pumping fun.

www.grendonlakes.co.uk

Nene White Water Centre
Get your wetsuit on and bounce down the rapids at Northamptonshire's premiere water sport venue.

Evening
www.nenewhitewatercentre.co.uk

FINISH

CAMBRIDGESHIRE

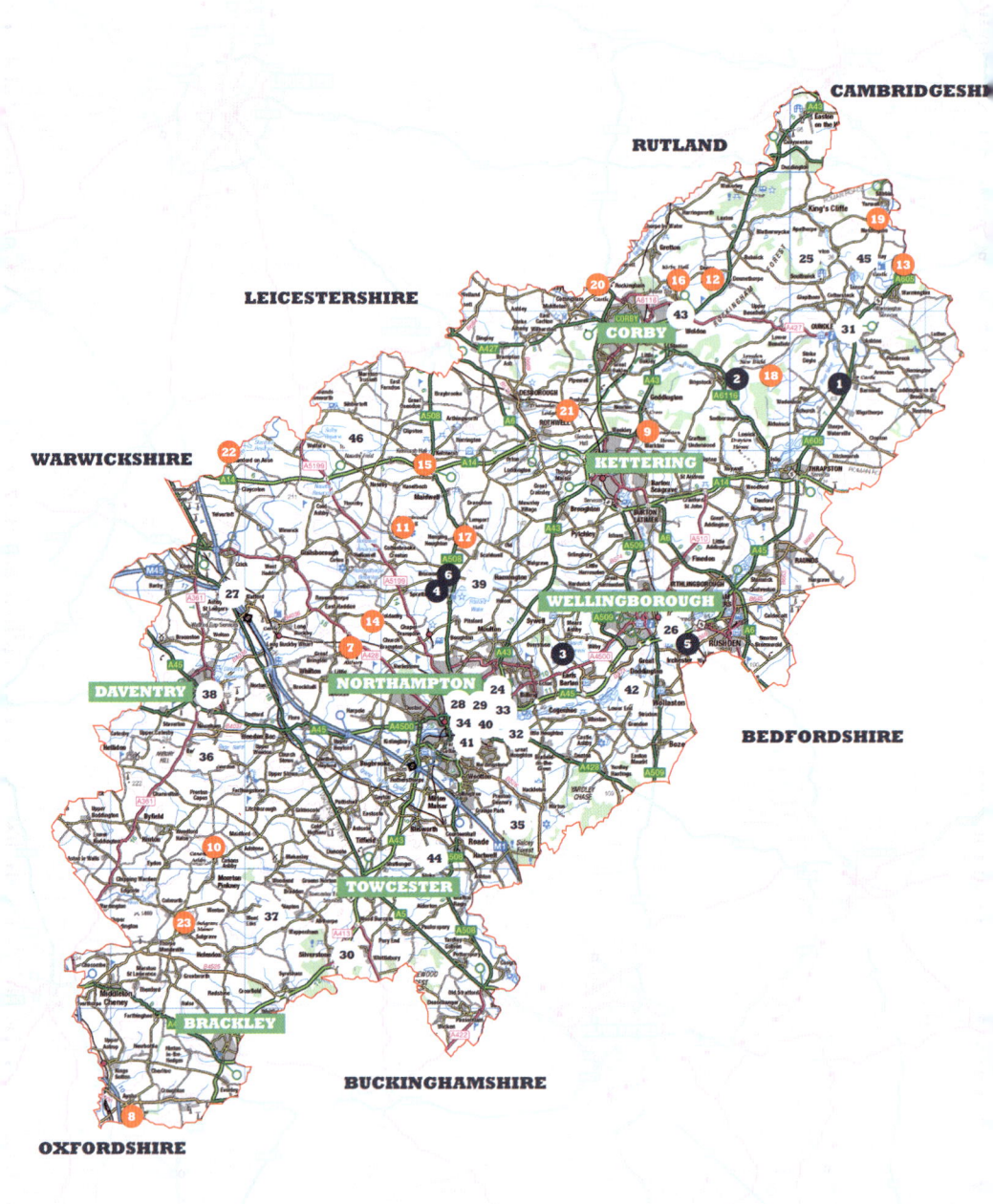

RUTLAND

LEICESTERSHIRE

WARWICKSHIRE

CORBY

KETTERING

WELLINGBOROUGH

BEDFORDSHIRE

DAVENTRY

NORTHAMPTON

TOWCESTER

BRACKLEY

BUCKINGHAMSHIRE

OXFORDSHIRE

Map not to scale